SHOULD YOU SHUT YOUR EYES WHEN YOU KISS?

SHOULD YOU SHUT YOUR EYES WHEN YOU KISS?

or
How to Survive
"The Best Years of Your Life"

by Carol McD. Wallace

Illustrated by Martha Weston

An Atlantic Monthly Press Book
Little, Brown and Company
BOSTON   TORONTO

FIRST EDITION

Library of Congress Cataloging in Publication Data

Wallace, Carol, 1955–
  Should you shut your eyes when you kiss? or, How to
survive "the best years of your life".

  "An Atlantic Monthly Press book."
  1. Youth—Life skills guides. 2. Students—Life
skills guides. 3. Youth—Family relationships. I. Title.
HQ796.W235   1983   646.7'0088055   83–5458
ISBN 0–316–91999–3

ATLANTIC-LITTLE, BROWN BOOKS
ARE PUBLISHED BY
LITTLE, BROWN AND COMPANY
IN ASSOCIATION WITH
THE ATLANTIC MONTHLY PRESS

VB

*Published simultaneously in Canada
by Little, Brown & Company (Canada) Limited*

PRINTED IN THE UNITED STATES OF AMERICA

To my sisters,
Eve and Josephine,
who were successful kids,
and are successful grown-ups

Acknowledgment

With heartfelt thanks to
Melanie Kroupa, who is
everything an editor
is supposed to be

CONTENTS

SCHOOL

AVOIDING IT

There are days in the life of every student when it is not only undesirable, but actually impossible, to go to school. Unfortunately, these days do not always fall on a Saturday, and do not always coincide with a bona fide illness. Thus it becomes necessary to take imaginative action. The official word for this is "malingering"—it's more often known as "playing sick."

You have to be careful about acting ill; you don't want to do it so often that your parents get suspicious, nor do you want them thinking you're a hypochondriac. The attitude to adopt is one of brave suffering—yes, yes, you're in pain but you *must* go to school. Pretend that the last thing in the world you want is to stay in bed. Let your parents know that you're hiding from them the terrible truth of just *how* awful you feel.

While you're at it, think big—and plan ahead. Do you have tests in two subjects a day apart next week? Start to get sick a day in advance—go to school but act listless. Pick at your dinner. Smile wanly at your siblings when they tease you. Don't *say* you're sick; wait for someone to notice. The next day, just lie in bed and exhibit the symptoms of your favorite disease.

REASONS NOT TO GO TO SCHOOL

Check off the ones that apply, and add them up. Subtract one point for every day of school you've missed in the last month. If you end up with more than three points, it could be that you should stay home.

— a test

— a test you haven't studied for

— a boring special assembly

— homework left undone

— a report due

— pimples

— a test being handed back

— a terrible lunch menu

— nothing to wear

Looking Sick

Anyone entering your bedroom should be confronted by you in bed, with the following props.

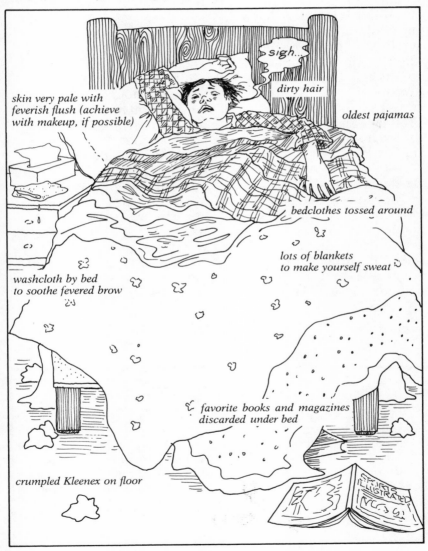

Stomach Ills:

A nervous stomach could be very useful, especially if you don't mind making yourself throw up. Better yet, learn to imitate the process (be sure to pour a glass of water into the toilet while you're making choking noises) and do so with the bathroom door slightly ajar. You don't need to fake a temperature, or swollen glands. Stomach illness can flare up any time. (You can also use it as a good excuse for not eating foods you don't like.)

Headaches:

They may sound paltry, but don't be deceived: if you can acquire a tendency to migraines you're golden. Describe flashing lights behind your eyes and a feeling of nausea, and walk around with an ice pack on your forehead. Migraine headaches are debilitating and mysterious; nobody really knows what causes them. Because they *are* so mysterious, any pattern of recurrence is feasible.

Your Generic Virus:

A chancy way of going about playing sick, but certainly creative. The crucial element should be a fever, so be sure you have a way of fixing the thermometer with no one looking. Tried and true methods include putting the thermometer on a radiator, on a hot water bottle, in a cup of tea. . . . Aim for a temperature between 100° and 104°— if you get higher than that, you're suddenly critically ill, and they may rush you off to the emergency room, which could be embarrassing.

CRUCIAL DON'TS

To be really convincing, you will have to effect some behavior modification. **Don't** show interest in anything. **Don't** rise to your siblings' baiting. **Don't** eat much at first; and when you do, make sure they all know you're "recovering." Make a point of refusing to eat your favorite things. **Don't** try to get away with staying home from school and then going to a party. That's a dead giveaway.

GETTING TO SCHOOL

This is a game you can play with yourself every day.

You leave the house on time	− 2		
You forget your books	+ 1		
your homework	+ 3		
your lunch	− 3		

You leave the house on time   − 2

You forget your books   + 1

  your homework   + 3

  your lunch   − 3

*You arrive first on the corner
to wait for the bus*   − 2

You arrive as the bus pulls up   + 2

*You arrive as the bus pulls
away*   0

*You stick out your thumb and
get a ride immediately*   + 3

  *with a 16-year-old member
of the opposite sex*   + 5

  who doesn't have acne   + 8

  who drives a foreign car   + 10

*The person without acne in a
foreign car passes you, yelling
something derisive*   − 5

You stick out your thumb and

finally get a ride

  with the school janitor   + 2

  with the school principal   − 4

  with your father   − 8

*You walk to the next intersection where there's a candy
store and a phone*   + 1

*You use your only dime to call
your mother*   − 5

*You use your only dime to call
the school*   − 7

*You use your lunch money to
buy a candy bar and a copy
of* Playboy   + 8

*You talk the owner of the
candy store into driving you
to school*   + 15

*You walk all the way to school
and arrive late*   − 2

*You had a test first period
anyway*   + 4

SCORING

0 – 10: Relax. Even Einstein missed classes now
and then.

10 – 20: Right on target.

Over 20: Caution! You'll never make it through the
year at this rate.

CLASSROOM BEHAVIOR

The goal of classroom behavior is to make sure the teacher understands at all times who is boss. You don't want to show direct animosity, and you don't want to do anything you can be punished for. But your teachers should always know that if you are listening, it's as a personal favor.

DOS	DON'TS
draw	*raise your hand*
pass notes	*take notes*
chew gum	*listen*
read comics	*follow in the book*
fidget	*volunteer to read out loud*

THINGS TO DO TO DRIVE A TEACHER CRAZY THAT CAN'T REALLY GET YOU IN TROUBLE

• Yawn constantly. Cover your mouth so it looks like you're trying to be polite.
• Call the teacher *just* the wrong name: "McGill" instead of "McGraw," for instance. Once in a blue moon, get the name right.
• Stare.
• Stare and drool slightly.

You will, of course, be called on to answer questions from time to time; when the teacher calls your name and asks you directly, there is no way to get out of it. In the unlikely event that you know the answer to the question, you have only to produce it, in as few words as possible. However, it is more probable that you won't know the answer. You may not even have heard the question.

• Never ask a teacher to repeat a question. Ask him to "rephrase" it.

• If you did hear the question, but don't know what the teacher's talking about, say that you don't really understand its significance relative to the matter at hand. Maybe you'll pick up a hint or two when he explains.

• If you know *something* about what the teacher's discussing, but simply don't have the answer to that particular question, dismiss it by saying, "I actually think it's more important to look into . . ." and talk about something you're familiar with.

• If you can't think of a thing to say, admit that you haven't read the material. It's better to look unprepared than to look stupid.

Time spent in a classroom is really the ideal time to pass notes. Note-passing keeps open the lines of communications between friends. Some notes, of course, are confidences between best friends and should be kept secret. It is not, however, necessarily disastrous if a note falls into the wrong hands, providing that the contents aren't too compromising.

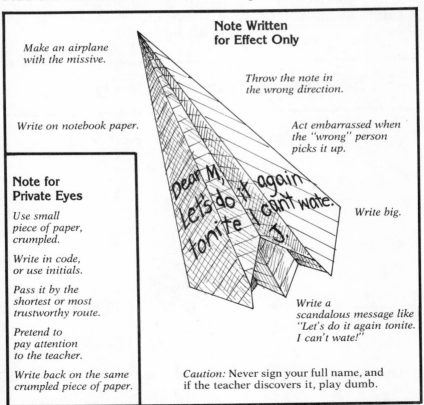

Make an airplane with the missive.

Note Written for Effect Only

Throw the note in the wrong direction.

Write on notebook paper.

Act embarrassed when the "wrong" person picks it up.

Note for Private Eyes

Use small piece of paper, crumpled.

Write in code, or use initials.

Pass it by the shortest or most trustworthy route.

Pretend to pay attention to the teacher.

Write back on the same crumpled piece of paper.

Write big.

Write a scandalous message like "Let's do it again tonite. I can't wate!"

Caution: Never sign your full name, and if the teacher discovers it, play dumb.

TEACHERS

THINGS TEACHERS
DO
THAT DRIVE ALL
STUDENTS CRAZY

- calling you "young people"

- instead of getting mad, saying, "I'm disappointed in you"

- telling you what a *wonderful* time of life you're going through

- using outdated slang

- trying to get you to tell them things: "Is everything all right at home?"

- making class work "meaningful"

The Classic Types, Illustrated

THE YOUNG FEMALE
ENGLISH TEACHER

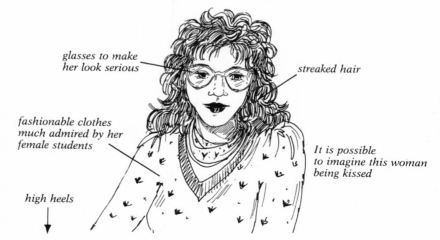

glasses to make her look serious

streaked hair

fashionable clothes much admired by her female students

It is possible to imagine this woman being kissed

high heels

THE GYM TEACHER

short hair, cut like Brillo

whistle

blue sweatshirt
(she owns them in grey
and green, too)

bermuda shorts

amazing calf muscles

white sneakers,
always clean

impossible to imagine
her being kissed

THE MATH TEACHER

Still uses Brylcreem

black-framed glasses

polyester short-sleeved shirt

high-water pants

crepe-soled oxfords
that look as much
like black sneakers
as possible

CHAPERONE
FOR THE DANCE

hair freshly done
in curly helmet style

sparkly glasses
for evening wear

corsage she
sent herself

upholstered in
powder blue brocade
from 1950

little purse for
Kleenex, mouth spray,
red lipstick

silver high heels;
inside, toenails
painted red

9

SLEEPING IN CLASS

There are so many terrific things to do late at night that it's a wonder anyone ever gets to sleep. The drawback to staying up all night is that it means a person has to sleep during the day, and as the most appealing time to sleep is when nothing interesting is going on—this means in class.

GOOD OPPORTUNITIES

slide shows or movies

lectures

tests, if you finish early or know you're going to fail anyway

study periods

DANGEROUS

labs

classes with fewer than 15 people

extra-help sessions

1. Sit at the back, out of the teacher's line of vision.

2. Never put your head down on your desk—you will never convince *anyone* that you're just thinking.

3. Keep a book open in front of you. When your eyes are open, your gaze should fall directly on the page.

4. Keep your mouth shut; a slack jaw is a dead giveaway.

5. Don't drool.

Staying Awake

Sometimes, of course, you have to stay awake. Maybe you can't get away with sleeping, or maybe you need to hear what the teacher's saying so that you can pass the course.

1. Sit near an open window so that you're so cold you couldn't possibly sleep. (Catch pneumonia, yes. Sleep, no.)

2. Pinch yourself, chew the inside of your cheek, clench your leg muscles. That will wake you up momentarily.

3. Think about something pleasant and exciting, like kissing the prettiest girl in the room.

4. Think about being in an embarrassing situation, like getting a traffic ticket, or being pinched on the fanny.

HOW TO ACT SMART

Although it's a ruling principle of adolescence that no one should stand out from the crowd, being remarkable can have certain advantages. For instance, if you can convince your teachers that you're exceptionally smart, after a while they'll give you better grades automatically. They will probably forgive eccentric behavior, excusing it on the grounds of your intelligence. If you're lucky they may even let you off from class to do an independent study, supposedly taking greater advantage of your presumed talents.

1. Cultivate an interest, and let everyone know about it. Choose something obscure like Tibetan art or frog breeding, and get obsessive about it—obsession is very intellectual.

2. Don't do the assigned school reading—but dabble in something related. If you're supposed to be reading *A Tale of Two Cities*, read a biography of Dickens or a history of the French Revolution in-

stead. (You can skim.) Dominate the class discussion with anecdotes about the Bastille or what Dickens ate for breakfast.

3. Use big words. It doesn't really matter if you can't spell or pronounce them correctly, but you'd better know what they mean, because people will ask. When you're right, they'll think you're a prodigy.

4. Don't talk much. Instead, talk *selectively*. Make up complete sentences in your mind and drop them into conversation when there's a pause. They should be grammatically perfect and contain at least one polysyllabic word.

DOING YOUR
HOMEWORK

The basic premise to doing homework is simple; you should do anything to get out of reading and writing. Reading and writing demand attention and effort; they cannot be accomplished while watching TV or talking on the phone. Fortunately, teachers can be duped by shows of arts and crafts. If you consistently hand in models or collages instead of reports, they will call you "creative" and say you should be an architect. If you always want to put on a play or skit, they'll say you should go on the stage. Either way, you get out of real intellectual labor.

Unfortunately, you can't always fool the teacher. Sometimes you have to really work. The trick then is to enlist your family's help.

Below are some lines to use: match them up with the appropriate person to use them on. If you get them all right, you probably don't need to be reading this book anyway.

MIX AND MATCH	
Younger Sibling	Our English teacher wants us to write about our most interesting memories. I think that's a neat project: can you remember what your most interesting memory is?
Mom	Did you have Miss Oglethorpe? Did she give you a test on irregular verbs conjugated with "être"? Do you still have it? How much do you want for it?
Dad	If you don't color this map for me I'll tell Mom about the night you snuck out. . . .
Older Sibling	Hey, I've got this really interesting math problem I want you to see.

NOT DOING YOUR HOMEWORK

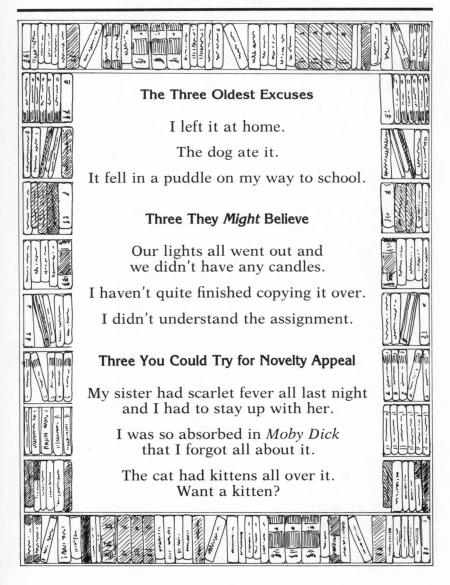

The Three Oldest Excuses

I left it at home.

The dog ate it.

It fell in a puddle on my way to school.

Three They *Might* Believe

Our lights all went out and
we didn't have any candles.

I haven't quite finished copying it over.

I didn't understand the assignment.

Three You Could Try for Novelty Appeal

My sister had scarlet fever all last night
and I had to stay up with her.

I was so absorbed in *Moby Dick*
that I forgot all about it.

The cat had kittens all over it.
Want a kitten?

WRITING REPORTS

THE PERFECT REPORT

Pick an obscure topic. With luck, your teacher will know nothing about it—with even more luck, you won't be able to find anything out about it at all, which is the perfect excuse for not writing anything.

Use pictures. If you can find them, cut appropriate photographs out of magazines. Or use inappropriate photographs, and write clever captions. Trace pictures and color them in. Glue them carefully onto notebook paper, one picture per page.

Copy the report over (but don't type it unless you want to be branded a nerd forever). Use ink and be neat. Space your letters and your words far apart, and make wide margins.

Buy a neat cover, with a catchy title in handsome lettering. Put the teacher's name on the cover, too; everyone likes to see their name in print.

Use lots of paper; include a title page, a table of contents, and a blank page at the back that says "Notes."

Make a bibliography, to show where you got your information. Do not list your father, or your sister's last year's history paper. Do list every book the library had on the subject, even if you only looked at one.

INTERESTING TOPICS

The First Defenestration of Prague (three guys got thrown out a window and it started a war)

Bubonic plague

Genghis Khan or Attila the Hun

Roman banquets and orgies

The eruption of Krakatoa

Recyling

You may have the techniques for *writing* reports down to a science, but there's one more principle that will make your life much easier: Never use material just once. Recycle everything: research, pictures, even complete reports. In the old days, ladies used to take the old ribbons and flowers off hats and put on new ones and pretend they had completely new headgear. You can do the same with schoolwork.

Say, for example, you wrote a report on Impressionism for history class. You put in illustrations (art postcards) and lots of references, giving the artists' full names and birth-dates to fill up the page. You can change the identity of this (say, to a report on Monet for art class) with a few simple alterations.

1. Illustrations should always be glued onto separate pages so you can take out the postcards of Seurat and replace them with reproductions of the "Waterlilies."

2. Don't bother copying over the whole report. Just add a page or two about Monet's life and paintings. Consider the rest "background." Use the same pen.

3. A new title page is essential. Invent a catchy new title and put on it, "For Art 8B, Mrs. Samgrass, November 18," to personalize the report.

N.B.: You can use this one project for several more purposes—it can become a report on French nineteenth-century painters for French class, a report on Paris and the surrounding countryside for geography. You can do a little more research now and then to add a few new facts—if you play your cards right, this one paper could even get you through college!

THUMBNAIL PLOTS

Romeo and Juliet:
Juliet is thirteen. Romeo is fifteen. They live in Italy a long time ago and their parents don't like each other. He climbs in her window one night. They both die in the end.

Great Expectations:
Pip meets a convict in a graveyard. Somebody decides to make him a gentleman so he goes to London. He meets a girl named Estella who is very mean to him. Miss Havisham is Estella's aunt and she lives in a big old creepy house. She never got married and her wedding cake is still there, full of spiders.

Jane Eyre:
Jane is a little mousy governess who falls in love with her employer. She finally has to run away and when she comes back years later he is blind and loves her. His first wife was crazy in the attic the whole time.

The Great Gatsby:
The Great Gatsby is a very rich man who lives on Long Island in a house with a dock. He owns many shirts, and gives lots of parties. He also goes to New York wearing a huge pair of glasses. His wife Daisy plays a lot of golf.

Robinson Crusoe:
Robinson was shipwrecked on an island all by himself. He was pretty bored until one Friday a Swiss family landed on the island and he adopted them. Then they built a big tree house and rode around the island on pigs.

The Old Man and the Sea:
An old fisherman goes out in his boat to catch a fish after he hasn't caught any in months. He hooks a really big one but it gets away and when he goes home and shows his family how big it was, they all say "Oh, sure" and don't believe him.

The Picture of Dorian Gray:

Dorian Gray is a very handsome fellow who has his portrait painted. He has some friends who are shady characters and they turn him on to drugs. (In those days they didn't smoke dope but opium, which is very expensive, so you had to be really rich to get high.) He gets older but he doesn't look it, only the portrait. Finally he gets tired of looking twenty (even though they didn't have things like legal drinking ages in those days), and he stabs the portrait.

Huckleberry Finn:

Huck Finn lived in Missouri with his friend Tom Sawyer, a fence-painter. Nobody ever taught him to speak English correctly, so he hangs out with a Negro slave named Jim. They run away together on a raft. Huck likes to play dress-up and pretend he's other people—first he pretends he's a girl and then he pretends he's Tom Sawyer. Jim can't pretend because he's a runaway now and besides he's in jail. In the end Tom saves them, but Huck still can't speak English.

RESPECTABLE DIRTY BOOKS

The following are well-known books that you can find on the shelves of any library. What they have in common is that they contain some rather explicit passages about sex. If you want to take them out, be careful; otherwise the librarian and your parents will know exactly why you wanted to read them. You can try to camouflage the key titles by checking them out along with other books. If, for instance, the author has written anything else, select two or three extra volumes so the librarian merely thinks you're a D. H. Lawrence buff. Or add a biography or critical study so you look like a young Joyce scholar. At home, keep the *interesting* book in the middle of the stack, and your parents may overlook it completely.

Ulysses

Lady Chatterley's Lover

Portnoy's Complaint

Tropic of Capricorn

The Group

The Canterbury Tales
(The Miller's Tale)

THE FIELD TRIP

It's a little hard to figure out why schools have field trips; you would think they would catch on that nobody pays attention to what you are supposed to see. Even if your teacher assigns a report on it, you all know that the main attraction of the trip is not culture, or science, or supplementing your classroom studies. It's skipping school, with permission. Of course, certain variables do make the trip more enjoyable.

• You forge your best friend's father's signature on the permission slip.

• You get on the bus with the cute teacher.

• You sit next to your best friend, in a window seat *or*

• You sit in the back, where you sneak cigarettes.

• You get right up in the front of the group so you can pat the snake/ get the actor's autograph/ touch the picture frame to make the alarm go off.

• You get separated from the group and get to see the snake's dinner (a dead rat)/ the dressing room/ the museum guards necking.

• The object of the field trip includes a picture, a statue, or a dummy of a woman with bare breasts.

• The object of the field trip includes a picture, a statue, or a dummy of a naked man.

• You make loud cracks about the other school groups ("What a bunch of wimps") until their teacher yells at your teacher.

• You have enough money to buy several hot dogs and candy bars for the bus ride home.

• You pretend to get carsick and have to stop the bus.

• The teacher forgot to count and you lose someone.

• You get lost on the way home.

• The bus breaks down.

LUNCH

Matching Quiz: Lunch Style

The cafeteria is a real microcosm of school society, and even choices of food tend to correspond with personality. See if you can match the following types to the meals they've chosen: you'll find that two of the people ate the same lunch!

Perpetual Dieter	*Brings lunch in aluminum lunch box. Contents: tuna fish sandwich, Thermos of milk, apple. Peels apple. Throws wax paper from sandwich carefully in garbage.*
Nerd	*Brings lunch from home in plastic bags tucked into purse. Contents: carrot sticks, boiled egg. Buys diet soda from vending machine—decides to sneak cigarette instead of eating.*
Jock	
Popular Girl	*Buys cafeteria lunch: soup, hamburger, potato chips, cake, milkshake. Eats it all, fast. Buys two candy bars for "dessert."*
Greaser	*Buys cafeteria lunch: potato chips and Twinkies. Eats them idly, thinking about more important things, like sex.*

Safest Choices

Cafeteria food is terrible, but in some schools it's considered queer to bring lunch from home, so you have to pick your meal from what the steam tables offer. To be safe:

1. Forget a balanced diet. That's what you eat at home.

2. Go for food that was made somewhere else and brought in, sealed. Like milk, ice cream bars, potato chips.

3. The next safest stuff is cold: sandwiches, coleslaw.

4. Stay away from hot food except vegetables (but who wants to eat vegetables any-way?). You have no idea what gross ingredients they might put in the gravy.

5. Examine the food before you eat it—open the sandwich. Look for rubber bands under the lettuce. Stir up your soup to see if there's anything weird floating in the bottom.

6. Believe *every* story you hear about the Mafia grinding up their victims in the hot dogs and somebody once finding a southern-fried mouse with the chicken wings. It could happen to you.

LOCKERS

Lockers are one of the best reasons for going to public school. In private school you don't usually get one, and have to carry all your things around in a bag. Someone should point out to private school headmasters that they are probably warping their students by depriving them of a major form of self-expression.

You've been told that you are what you eat, and you know that your clothes say a lot about you. So does your school locker: what you have in it, how neat it is, what's pasted to the inside of the door.

Locker Content

STUDENT COUNCIL MEMBER

extra stockings in case of a run

Kleenex

Band-Aids

paper punch for keeping ring binder in order

ruler

spare notebooks

minutes from student council meeting

JOCK

2 mitts, favorite and second-best

last 3 issues of Sports Illustrated

tin of Cruex

driver's manual for 1972 Mustang

Trojans

3-month-old Penthouse, cover torn off

spare pair of sneakers

1 dirty tube sock

team jacket, crumpled up

ON THE DOOR

Acceptable

mirror: cracked,
for a vain jock;
with cute frame for
a popular cheerleader

Doonesbury cartoons

photos of Cheryl Tiegs
(in wet bathing suit
or T-shirt),
David Bowie, Rex Smith, Tom Selleck

Unacceptable

cute pictures
of animals

maps

your class schedule

Hopelessly Outdated

Peter Max posters, Shaun Cassidy,
Farrah Fawcett

by Personality Type

MATH WHIZ   POPULAR GIRL

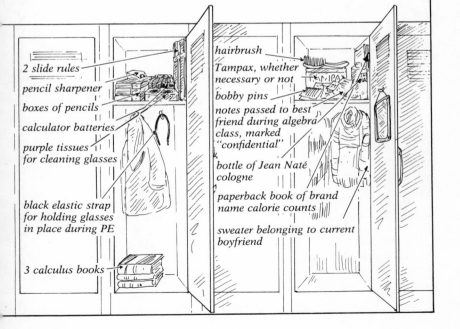

2 slide rules

pencil sharpener

boxes of pencils

calculator batteries

purple tissues
for cleaning glasses

black elastic strap
for holding glasses
in place during PE

3 calculus books

hairbrush

Tampax, whether
necessary or not

bobby pins

notes passed to best
friend during algebra
class, marked
"confidential"

bottle of Jean Naté
cologne

paperback book of brand
name calorie counts

sweater belonging to current
boyfriend

HOW ATHLETIC ARE YOU?

One of the great shocks of junior high is the continuous institutional effort to rank students. Perhaps nowhere is this process as painful as in the gym, where, for the first time, the chosen few are designated as athletes and the rest as clods. It never hurts to be prepared for public humiliation; the following quiz should help you to figure out where you belong on the athletic spectrum.

My idea of a good workout is:

a. running three miles, doing fifty sit-ups, and playing two sets of tennis.
b. putting on my leotard, finding my *Saturday Night Fever* album, and touching my toes ten times to "Staying Alive."
c. walking to the refrigerator, opening it, removing and devouring three ice-cream sandwiches.

Your idea of a modern sports hero is:

a. Mean Joe Green.
b. Secretariat.
c. the girl who models the bathing suits for *Sports Illustrated*.

You are invited to go to an all-day picnic, and you know that a certain guy/girl you have a crush on will be there. You are instructed to bring your tennis racket because there will be a round robin. You:

a. Confidently look forward to playing, because your skill is sure to make you look good in your crush's eyes.
b. don't bring a racket, hoping that no busybody will offer to loan you theirs.
c. don't go. No crush is worth the embarrassment of having to play tennis in public, given the way you play.

In elementary school, when teams were chosen for games, you were always chosen:

a. first.
b. in the middle.
c. last.

Under the blanket is your Christmas present. If you had a choice, you'd pick:

a. a pair of skis, or other athletic equipment.
b. a dog, barking.
c. a six-pack of beer.

You are sitting in the stands at a baseball game. The batter hits a foul ball that heads right toward you. Instinctively, you:

a. stand on your seat and reach to catch it.
b. duck.
c. wonder whatever possessed you to go to a ball game of any kind.

Scoring

"a" answers indicate that you are well on your way to being a jock.
"b" answers mean that you are athletically competent, but certainly not a star.

"c" answers show that you are hopelessly unathletic. You will probably not be surprised to hear it.

SPORTS FOR JOCKS

OK, we all know you're good—you know you're good. You can play any sport you want. There are advantages and disadvantages to all of them.

Football

PRO

prestige

flattering uniforms

you play at Homecoming

team fellowship

CON

you can get hurt

training in summer

you never get to watch from the stands

you may warm a bench the whole season

Basketball

PRO

the perfect sport for really *tall people*

no playing outside in bad weather

lots of action for everyone

CON

it's hard unless you are *really tall*

gyms always smell

all that running up and down the court

Tennis

PRO

free coaching and court time

exposure to the boys' team/ the girls' team

no uniforms

CON

having to train for a sport everybody else just plays

playing in front of members of the opposite sex

those shorts are murder if your legs aren't great

Field Hockey

PRO

all that team spirit

whacking the ball with a stick gets rid of aggression

exercising in that crisp, exhilarating autumn air

CON

the team may never pass you the ball

getting yourself whacked in the shins hurts

you can freeze your tail off out on that field

Gymnastics

PRO	CON
you can show off with fun tricks like cartwheels	definitely not for the uncoordinated
you feel like you can fly on the rings and bars	what if you get airsick?
one sport that's perfect for the small-boned	leotards are not flattering to all bodies

Soccer

PRO	CON
both boys and girls can play, so you can show off	both boys and girls can play, so you may have to play in the presence of the opposite sex
everyone is capable of kicking a ball around a field	not quite everyone
it's a fast, exciting sport	you have to spend a solid hour running up and down a field

Wrestling

PRO	CON
nobody will ever give you a hard time	all that groping with other guys
great for body-building	no audience at the matches
you can keep your siblings under control	all the girls will think of you as muscle-bound

PROFILE OF THE SUPER-JOCK

- yells louder than the coach
- wouldn't miss any of the games, or even varsity, JV, and intramural practices
- will work up a sweat at a moment's notice
- owns six pairs of athletic shoes, each for a particular sport
- wears a whistle around his neck
- is always "in training"

PROFILE OF A CHEERLEADER

- always has clean hair
- is neither dumb nor smart
- is bright and energetic, even at 8 A.M.
- takes high school sports *completely* seriously
- shaves her legs twice a week
- never had braces
- always has a hairbrush in her purse

PROFILE OF THE CHRONICALLY UNCOORDINATED

- shuts his eyes when he tries to catch
- can bat left- or right-handed, will strike out either way
- gets out of breath walking down the aisle at the movies
- shows greatest coordination turning the pages of a book
- finally learned to ride a bike at age 12
- disappears when Frisbees are brought out at picnics

31

HOW TO SURVIVE PHYS ED

Some people actually like PE—they like to exercise, they like getting all sweaty in the middle of the day. If you're one of them, don't read this section; there are plenty of others for whom gym is the darkest part of the day.

Getting Excused

The best way to cope with PE, of course, is not to go at all. Unfortunately, gym teachers are pretty well accustomed to reluctant students. Be sure to avoid making the following mistakes:

1. Claiming that you have cramps more often than once a month

2. Faking a limp, and forgetting which foot is supposed to be hurt

3. Forging an excuse from a doctor for a disease that doesn't exist.

On the other hand, some evasive tactics may work simply on the strength of their boldness. Try:

1. Wearing an Ace bandage on your wrist for a "torn ligament." Ligaments heal *very slowly*. You can even take the bandage off and try to play too soon—and reinjure yourself. With luck this injury could become chronic and you'll never have to play again.

2. Telling the gym teacher that sports are against your religion. (Have a religion ready—Witnesses of God in the Human Body, for example.)

3. Getting your friends to sign in for you, and to cover. "Ann can't play first base; she had to go back to the gym to get her mitt." They can yell, "Go, Ann!" when other people are running a race, and "Ann just served" when they're rotating on the volleyball court.

Evasive Action

Eventually you probably will have to go to a gym class. This can be made a little more bearable, especially if you don't have to get sweaty.

1. Take the precaution of signing up for the least strenuous sport possible: archery, folk-dancing, rhythmic movement, that sort of thing. Avoid anything that requires a ball.

2. Make a habit of being a little bit late—so that you don't have enough time, for instance, to change into your gym suit.

3. If you do have to play, try to be placed where there will be no action: goalie, perhaps, or in the outfield.

4. Never *ever* catch a ball.

5. Keep having to adjust your equipment.

6. Volunteer to keep score.

SEX EDUCATION

There are a lot of things about institutionalized sex education that are funny, not the least of which is that, by the time *they* decide you're old enough to know about sex, you know everything anyway. What's more, your teachers try to be very discreet—they put on expressions that indicate that (1) they are *not* embarrassed and (2) they never do this sort of thing themselves. In fact, sex education at your school could be very dull; a movie about some poor clod of a 1950s teenager, a speech from the biology teacher in which he says "mature" a lot. However, you can spice up the proceedings considerably if you want to, by asking a few very specific questions. The dumber the question, the more embarrassing the response. For instance, try:

1. I caught my sister and her boyfriend making out on the couch. Why was his hand in her blouse?

2. Can you get pregnant from a toilet seat? (Especially effective at the end of all the speeches, when they've told you four times that you can't.)

3. If sex isn't dirty why does my father hide *Playboy* under the bed?

4. Were you a virgin when *you* got married?

5. What's orgasm?

THE SHOWERS

Fools may ask what is so bad about having to take a shower after gym. Ha! Give them seven minutes to complete the following obstacle course and get to class on time. Then they'll know.

1 Get your locker open in a hurry when you've forgotten the combination and the lock sticks. Oops, wrong locker. Try again.

2 Undress without looking stupid, like standing on one leg with your feet tangled in your underpants.

3 Wrap one of those miniature athletic towels around you so it covers everything important.

4 Walk from locker to shower *fast*, without slipping on the floor.

5 Wait for a free shower stall with everyone staring at you.

6 Everyone is bigger than you are.

35

THE DANCE: FINDING A DATE

It never fails: the person you want to ask to the dance is the good-looking athlete/cheerleader who sits next to you in English and asked you once what the assignment was. The one you end up asking is the son/daughter of your mother's best friend that you have Thanksgiving with every year. Your mother insists that he/she will "grow into his/her looks."

GOLDEN RULE

The girl is always taller than the boy.

Asking: You will need, first, to discuss your choice of a date with all of your friends, to make sure that (a) they approve of your choice and (b) nobody else asks him or her first. The best way to ask someone is at school. Start thinking about it several days in advance, so that you have plenty of time to chicken out—not once but several times. It is essential that your approach seem completely casual; there just happens to be this dance and you don't have anything else to do on that night and your friends all seem to be going so do you want to come along? The following conditions are neces-sary for the actual asking: you must not be alone, but none of your friends should wit-ness the conversation, and circumstances must not make it necessary for you to sit there talking. A fast getaway is es-sential.

Asking by Telephone: Unfor-tunately, not everyone goes to school with members of the opposite sex, and even those who do may want to (or need to) ask someone they don't see every day. This involves use of the telephone.

Telephoning requires de-tailed advance planning. First the conversation has to be re-hearsed: identifying yourself, exchanging pleasantries, asking the big question. Writing it out might not hurt—in several versions to allow for some variation on the response.

QUIT WHEN YOU'RE AHEAD:

The conversation may run like this: "Hi. This is Bob. Bob Ahern? You know, I sat next to you in typing last summer? You don't know? . . ." Hang up and try to pretend it never happened.

You also have to pick a good time to call. Having a parent answer the phone is undesirable, but having a sibling answer it is even worse. However, the real disaster would be to make the phone call, get a sibling who tells you that X isn't there, and to have to call back. This might be grounds for coming up with a whole new choice of date. Back to square one.

HOW TO ASK FOR A DATE ON THE PHONE

1. Do a few push-ups or toe touches to get warmed up.
2. Sit down for ten minutes and tell yourself what a coward you are and how silly you're being.
3. Tell yourself that you must make this phone call by a certain deadline: before two o'clock, before your mother comes home from the supermarket, before dinner.
4. Pick up the phone and dial a few times, but hang up before dialing the last number.
5. Call a friend for coaching. Promise to call the date right away, and to call your friend right back to report.
6. Dial the whole number.
7. Let it ring once, and hang up in panic.
8. Repeat steps 2–6.

THE DANCE: GETTING THROUGH IT

Lining up a date for a dance is probably the worst part of the whole affair, but even when you've nailed down a date, you're not out of the woods. You still have to worry about what to wear, how to get there, and if you'll make it through the evening. The goal, of course, in all three areas, is to look as old as possible, and to act cool. (Girls, unfortunately, also have to worry about looking pretty.) But above all, you want to *blend in*.

The Perfect Couple   The More Likely Couple

WHAT TO WEAR

Keep it simple. A dance is not the time to try anything fancy like:

- shaving for the first time (face or legs).

- wearing a brand new pair of shoes.

- trying to get out of the house with a lot of makeup on.

- wearing a strapless dress.

- trying a new brand of deodorant.

HOW TO GET THERE

There are *ways* and *ways*. In order of preference:

1. with a friend who, owing to some stroke of fate, has reached his sixteenth birthday before finishing ninth grade. (He may not be too smart, but who cares at a time like this?)

2. with an older sibling; your favorite older sibling. Remember that this will put you completely at this sibling's mercy for weeks to come.

3. with a parent. Your mother may be more tactful, but a father looks a lot less babyish.

Of course, if by a miracle you live in a city with taxis, you have the advantages of mobility, independence, and privacy. Presumably you know how lucky you are.

EVEN THE BEST-LAID PLANS . . .

• A huge pimple grows on your chin. When you try to pop it, you only make it worse.

• Your brother doesn't leave the ball game in time, so your father has to take you.

• Your mother decides to come too.

• The sedan won't start, so you have to take the car with the Kitty Litter in the back.

• You're early. You have to come in and talk to your date's parents. So do your parents.

• You bought a pin-on corsage; everyone else at the dance has wrist corsages.

• The band is playing slow music when you get there and you can't find any of your friends.

• You forget your date's name.

• It's a costume dance and you aren't in costume.

• An hour later the band is still playing slow music. You ask your date to dance and she says "no."

• Your date never asks you to dance.

• You finally dance and step all over your date's feet.

• Your parents come to watch you.

• Your date has ditched you for someone who's two inches shorter and has worse acne.

• Your brother comes to pick you up and asks in a loud voice if you want him to go park somewhere for a while.

40

FAMILY

ADJUSTING YOUR ATTITUDE

SOME CONSIDERATIONS
THAT
MAY HELP TO MAKE YOUR
OTHER RELATIVES
BEARABLE

1. They divert your parents' attention from you, at least part of the time. Your mother would probably prefer talking to her sister on the phone to yelling at you.

2. They're good for telling stories about. Everyone has some peculiar relatives who do things that make other people laugh. Grandmothers are the best source for these stories; they know everything, and they're not afraid to tell.

3. They can remind you that at least you didn't get the family nose or red hair.

4. They make a nice crowd around the table at holidays, and everybody knows you can get away with more in a crowd.

5. Maybe you can borrow money from them.

THINGS YOU
CAN ALWAYS COUNT
ON YOUR PARENTS FOR

1. They will stand up for you in any argument against an outsider.
2. They will bail you out of jail.
3. They will remember that you love corn on the cob and hate peas.
4. They will come to watch you sing with the All-State Choir, even if they can't possibly see you in the crowd.
5. They never forget your birthday.
6. They think you are handsome, or beautiful, even if you know you aren't.
7. They will buy gas at your gas station, or bank at your bank, or go to your branch of the post office, as long as you work there.
8. They will really make an effort to like the man/woman you marry.
9. They will even babysit for your children someday. Free.

DINNER TABLE
BEHAVIOR

CONVERSATION: A GAME

Below are various sentences which, when strung together, pass for conversation. Put them in order, attribute them to the correct speaker, and see how accurate you are when dinner rolls around.

____ Mom, can I wear lipstick every day?

____ What would you say to a camping trip in July?

____ Guess who Susie has a crush on?

____ Ow!

____ Eat your peas.

____ No, you may *not*.

____ I got an 85 on the science test.

____ Did you hear about the Jacksons' baby?

____ Stop kicking me!

____ *Please* use your knife and fork.

____ Matthew, your dog has . . .

Investigate the food on the dinner table carefully. You never know when any of the following may have been cleverly disguised:

liver
lima beans
parsnips
beef tongue
buttermilk
spinach
cooked carrots
brussels sprouts

HOW TO AVOID EATING

Your parents may still insist that you eat everything on your plate. You are clearly too old for this, and they clearly have the upper hand. The answer, then, is to manage to get the food *off* your plate somehow—but not necessarily into your mouth.

If you know ahead of time that you aren't going to want to eat dinner, stick a Baggie into your pocket before you get to the table. This saves wear and tear on the clothes, and makes it a lot easier to dispose of the evidence.

Better yet, if you have a dog, this is one of the places where he comes in very handy—as a live-in, furry, four-footed garbage disposal. However, it's worth remembering that not everything you feed him may agree with him, and that if he gets sick, you will probably have to clean it up. Never *ever* feed a dog chicken bones.

1. For crumbly or mushy food (overcooked hamburgers, mysterious casseroles), dissect and disperse on plate.

2. For solid, fairly durable food (green beans, chicken wings), remove wholesale into lap.

HOW TO SURVIVE A FAMILY VACATION

It sounded like fun when your father first mentioned it. You've been excited about this vacation for weeks. As you get into the car with your parents and siblings, you suddenly realize the big catch—you have to spend the whole vacation with your family. There are ways to make this bearable.

On an Airplane:
Try to sit away from the rest of the family. Make a big stink about getting a seat next to the window, or over the wing, or close to the movie screen. Once you're there, don't make the mistake of trying to get friendly with the person next to you. You will immediately be reprimanded for making a pest of yourself and forced to trade places with your sister.

In a Car:
Sleep as much as you possibly can. Refuse to participate in the dopey games (like "I Packed My Grandmother's Trunk") that your mother

46

thinks make the trip go faster. Insist that you sit next to the window because you feel carsick, and threaten to throw up on your siblings when they get out of hand.

On the Street, in the Airport, at Disneyland:

Don't make the mistake of straying too far from the family. Your mother will instantly want to call the police or have you paged, and your parents won't let you out of their sight again. Better to walk along about ten feet behind them so nobody could mistake you for one of *them*.

There are also rewards to going on vacation with the family. One of the greatest is staying in motels. To guarantee that you and your siblings get a room to yourselves, you should learn to snore and grind your teeth. If your parents want you to sleep in with them, don't object—just make sure they don't get any sleep themselves. Once you're in a separate room with your siblings, you'll want to take advantage of every minute of sleeping in a place that isn't somebody's house. Explore all the features. If the bed has "Magic Fingers," try it out. See if you can get dirty movies on TV. Open all the drawers to see if there are Bibles or postcards of the motel in them; keep the postcards. Jump up and down on the double bed. Take long, hot showers and use all the towels. Don't put *anything* back where you found it.

47

SEX EDUCATION AT HOME

You can sometimes tell that they're working up to informing you about sex. It is usually Mom's idea. She has to talk Dad into telling his sons; she'll take care of the girls. But until it's settled there's a lot of arguing behind closed doors, and significant glances at the breakfast table.

You can do your parents a big favor by acting tolerant about this. You know there's nothing to be embarrassed about, and you know you're just about as well informed (if not quite as experienced) as they are. It would be an act of great kindness to let them get the whole matter off their chests. You can precipitate matters this way:

DO:

1. Take a book about "the facts of life" out of the library, and put it on your desk with a bookmark in it. Move the bookmark so it looks like you're reading the book.

2. Waylay one of your parents one day, book in hand. Say, "I was just reading this book, and I had a couple of questions I wanted to ask you." (Act casual, like you're talking about something as innocuous as pet food.)

3. Ask a couple of questions about tangential matters like comparative birth control methods or premarital sex in Victorian England.

4. Nod reassuringly and say, "Well, I guess I know what it's all about. I'll take this book back to the library now. Thanks."

DO NOT:

1. snicker, giggle, or blush. Remember, your parents are the ones who are embarrassed.

2. mention friends, acquaintances, or siblings who have done it, gotten pregnant, or had abortions.

3. ask about your parents' sex life.

4. indicate that any of this could in any way pertain to you.

HOW TO SURVIVE A FAMILY GATHERING

One of the great hoaxes of American civilization is the notion that families should have fun together. It seems obvious, though, (a) that families can't choose each other, (b) that if they could they wouldn't, and (c) that they spend too much time to-gether anyway. Be that as it may, it's tradition on holidays and birthdays and anniversaries—in fact, at any excuse—to summon the relatives from all the corners of the globe. The following strategies may make it easier to survive.

Either: Pay attention to the oldest person in the room. This will make you very popular with the old person and with the old person's young relatives who don't know what to say themselves. This person (your grandmother, your great-uncle, whoever) has no responsibility for your behavior, so you don't have to mind your manners with him. Get him to tell stories about things your parents won't talk about, like why your Aunt Tillie never married and how Grandpa lost all that money.

Or: Gang up with the young relatives. If there are enough of you (six is ample) and you sit in front of the television or run around the yard screaming en masse you are virtually uncontrollable. The reason for this is that any kid's parents are loath to admit in front of other parents that their offspring is unmanageable. Therefore nobody is going to lose face by yelling at you; they'll just pretend your behavior is perfectly normal.

Rules

1. Avoid your mother at any cost. If you even get near her she will want you to do something—pass the candy dish or sing your solo from the Spring Pageant or even just tuck in your shirt.

2. Don't do anything outrageous. Not only will you be punished severely for acting up in front of the relatives, *but*, even your misdemeanor is likely to pass into family legend; "Remember the Fourth of July party when Susie got caught smoking?" The story will be told for the rest of your life, whenever it will embarrass you most.

3. Don't make any enemies. Don't beat up on a cousin or slip a live mouse into an aunt's coat pocket or try out your newest dirty joke at the table. You're going to have to see these people again—and again and again, for the rest of your life. It'll be easier if they like you.

KID BREAKS 2 RULES IN 5 SECONDS.

CHORES: DIVISION OF LABOR

Sometimes it seems extremely unfair; in order to remain part of the household (at times a dubious reward), your parents demand that you perform certain chores. They call it "pulling your weight." Now, your response to this will vary according to your temperament.

Your mother asks you to empty the wastebaskets. You:

a. do so promptly, so you won't forget and she won't nag.

b. remember every time you throw something away, then forget about it. When she reminds you the third time, get huffy and do it.

c. empty them onto the floor.

It is generally your job to cook dinner, since your mother gets home late from work. If you had your way:

a. you would make spaghetti on Monday and eat it all week.

b. you would all go to McDonald's.

c. you would try out three new recipes in the same night; all for chocolate cake.

It has been mentioned to you that perhaps it's time to start ironing your own clothes.

Your response is to:

a. iron six shirts on Sunday night.

b. wear everything wrinkled.

c. take all your clothes that need to be ironed to a thrift store, and trade them in for interesting things in polyester.

Your father announces at dinner that on Saturday you are all going to stay at home to clean out the garage.

a. You sigh and make a face, but he knows and you know that you'll be there.

b. You sigh and make a face, and even though he reminds you six more times, he has to collar you on Saturday morning as you're on your way out to a ball game.

c. You "forget" and invite your two best friends over. When they find you working in the garage, it's easy enough to talk them into pitching in.

If your answers were all "*a*," you are probably known as the "reliable" one in the family. This will give you an enviable degree of independence. On the other hand, your parents are no dummies, and chances are that when something needs to be done around the house, they will ask you. You will always do it, no matter how mad it makes you. This is foolish; explain that you are tired of being the only one who really "pulls his weight" around the house. Crucial: Don't whine and don't get mad. Say, "I don't want to resent you." If that doesn't work, see to it that there are some things you just *can't do*. Develop an inability to do laundry, for instance. Once you've shrunk your mother's three favorite sweaters she'll be pretty reluctant to trust you to wash *anything*. Remember: if you don't know how to milk the cow, no one will ask you to.

If your answers are all "*b*," you probably mean well enough but are careless. You may get tired of having your mother remind you *every* day that you are supposed to clean the kitchen floor on Saturdays. If so, you should do one of two things: either get yourself lined up for chores you can't forget to do (like washing the dishes), or else volunteer for the big jobs. If you resign yourself to sacrificing a few days to painting your bedroom, for instance, you will get credit for it that will cancel out any number of unwashed windows or undusted shelves.

If your answers are all "*c*," you are either preoccupied or a real troublemaker. If the first is true, it's probably because you're concentrating on a cure for the common cold or a new all-media art form. You just *can't* remember to do things. On the other hand, if you're a troublemaker, why did you bother to read this far?

COSMETIC TRICKS
TO SHOW THAT
YOU HAVE
CLEANED

• Leave the broom out where your mother will trip over it. After you've vacuumed, change the filter bag. Throw the old one away where your mother's bound to see it, like in the bathroom wastebasket.

• When cleaning something that shows (a mirror, the copper bottom of a pot), leave the tiniest bit undone so that the "before and after" contrast is quite plain.

• Check with every member of the family before you wash the kitchen floor, making it plain that *you* are trying to make things convenient for *them*. Barricade yourself in the kitchen for at least two hours. (This is a good opportunity for some thorough investigation of what might be good to eat in the refrigerator.) For the next three days, scream, "Oh, my floor!" when anybody drops anything.

POST A SIGN.

Please Wipe your feet!

PUT THE MOP IN THE DOORWAY.

LEAVE CHAIRS ON THE TABLE TOP.

LEAVE A BUCKET OF FILTHY WATER.

CAVEAT

Beware of offers like this from your sibling: "Hey, I know you want to go to the movies Saturday. I'll do the dishes, and you can do them for me *next* Saturday."

This is a trap. The offer stems from advance knowledge, like that next Saturday night your mother's planning to cook her special meat pie that uses 89 different pots and pans.

THINGS YOUR PARENTS WILL WANT YOU TO LEARN THAT MAY COME IN HANDY (UNLIKELY THOUGH IT MAY SEEM)

- dancing to old-fashioned music
- how to change a tire
- how to make white sauce
- typing
- what clothes are likely to run when you wash them

THINGS YOUR PARENTS WILL WANT YOU TO LEARN THAT YOU WILL NEVER NEED TO KNOW

- how to make a campfire and boil water in the wilderness
- how to play the piano
- French
- how to make hospital corners on a bed
- the capitals of all fifty states

THINGS YOUR PARENTS WON'T BELIEVE ARE USEFUL

- putting out a candle with two fingers
- doing a flip on a trampoline
- flipping a bottle top across the room with two fingers
- blowing large bubbles with bubble gum
- writing your name backward

YOUR ROOM

Insuring Your Privacy

If a man's home can be his castle, then a teenager's room can be, too. Your room is lots more than a place to sleep— it's a place to daydream, to sulk, to plot, to play. It's also one of the few outlets you have to express yourself. Privacy is essential.

Above all, this means keeping your parents out, especially while you are gone. Your mother may say she was just putting your underwear away, but you never know. . . .

No need to be drastic about it at first; you can gently *suggest* that they stay out. If that doesn't work, you may want to progress to no-trespassing signs or booby traps, but they shouldn't be too radical. The bucket of water balanced on top of the door will probably suffice.

If you can't break them of their bad habits, they may insist on a parental right to enter, despite your pointing out that even the police need a search warrant. The answer, then, is to make the surroundings so unpleasant that they will keep their visits short. You might:

1. Paint your room a color they can't abide: black, for example, or purple. A parachute draped from the ceiling or a huge and rickety loft or any other threatening props that you can get your hands on will be helpful. A large bird, uncaged, or maybe a snake . . . you get the idea.

2. Maybe they insist on keeping the room neutral. Or maybe you don't want to live in a simulated jungle. Then perhaps you can get away with simply living in a *mess*. If you leave your room in disarray, your parents will probably just shut the door on it.

Labels in illustration:
- NO DUMPING
- State
- towels within easy reach of shower
- homework stacked by the week
- bedtime reading
- bedtime eating
- unmade bed: tell Mom you're airing it
- shirts worn once but good for another wearing
- why put away something you use every day?
- socks always stored under bed
- clean clothes in one pile
- dirty clothes in another

Maintenance

When your mother screams about the mess, a few swift steps will pacify her. Make your bed. Hang up the towels. Stack the books in neat piles. Shove everything else under the bed. When should you *really* clean? When something starts to smell.

SHARING A ROOM

Sharing a room is a strain, even for married couples (haven't you heard your mother yelling at your father to pick up his socks?). It's much worse, naturally, with a sibling you may not even like too much. Remember, though, what useful allies the two of you can be, and you'll realize how important it is to keep the peace between you. A contract like this one, which spells out your respective rights as roommates, may make it easier to survive.

I, _____,

and I, _____,
inasmuch as we are constrained by parental considerations to share
a room, do agree, in the interest of keeping the peace, to the
following:
I. *Territory:* the room is to be divided geometrically such that
each tenant may claim exactly one half of it. The divider may be
visible or invisible. Neutral territory shall include a right-
of—way to the bathroom and to the door.
    A. Within each tenant's territory, decoration and mainte-
nance shall be the sole responsibility and privilege of that tenant. Without express stipulation no tenant shall be required to
make the other's bed, clean, or otherwise alter the status quo.
This shall be made plain to parents and other authority figures.
    B. One tenant may not cross into the neighboring territory
without permission, whether or not the tenant is there.
    C. If closets and bureaus are shared, a similar strict par-
titioning of territory shall be effected.
II. *Property:* Certain articles—a stereo, books, sports equipment—may be designated as communal property, and a strict schedule of time—sharing shall be devised and adhered to.
III. *Conduct:* Certain rules of conduct may be agreed upon, gov-
erning such matters as lights—out, nature of the awakening mech-
anism, volume of the stereo.
IV. *The Bathroom:* Some agreement shall be reached as to the usage
patterns of the bathroom: i.e., who goes first in the morning,
arrangements for showers and the steaming of mirrors, and con-
tingency plans for running out of hot water.
    Signed, this_____day of_____

Witness(parent)   Sibling

Witness(friend)   Sibling

SLEEPING

Your parents probably see it as perverse, but your sleeping habits may change considerably once you hit your teens. They must be made to understand that you can no longer be told when you may and may not be asleep.

Reading under the Covers

Frankly, your parents should be grateful that you're reading at all. The fact that you like reading enough to lose sleep over it *should* have them hysterical with pleasure. They may not see it that way, though, so you should be prepared.

1. Rig a trap so that you can tell when they're coming near your room—something they'll knock over at least four feet outside your door, for instance.

2. Have a decoy book ready in case you *do* get caught, something like *Ivanhoe* that they really can't object to. For a real snow job, find out what their favorite books were when *they* were your age, and display prominently.

3. Invest in a small but powerful flashlight. There's no point in going blind.

4. Make a tunnel of the blankets so you get fresh air.

5. Remember to go to sleep at some point, or you'll be a zombie at school the next day.

Midnight Snacks

Of course half the reason for staying up really late is to make the consumption of midnight snacks possible—or even necessary. You don't want to get caught, though, and you don't want to leave evidence that you've been raiding the kitchen. This is supremely important if you're on a diet, or even slightly overweight. Your family is sure to be merciless if they think you're sneaking food.

1. Wait until everyone's asleep, and remember that your brother may be lying in wait to catch you in the act.

2. Shhh.

3. Make sure you know what's being planned for tomorrow night's dinner. It's mortifying to have your mother (a) discover it gone, and (b) accuse you of eating it.

4. If you make it a habit to help with the dishes, you'll know what's under all those mysterious plastic lids and pieces of tinfoil. You won't waste time peering into dish after dish of cold vegetables.

5. Make sure you leave things looking exactly the way you found them. Don't scrape all the icing off the cake or cut one whole leg off the chicken. Nibble, but disguise your nibblings.

6. Never finish anything. Someone is sure to say, "I know there was some chocolate ice cream in the freezer," and all eyes will swivel accusingly toward you.

7. Don't be dumb enough to leave dishes in the sink, unless you're absolutely sure you'll be up first in the morning.

8. If possible, make this a hit-and-run raid—get what you want, and take it back to bed. That way nobody will surprise you in the kitchen when *they* come downstairs for a midnight snack.

FOODS TO AVOID EATING IN BED:

Barbecue

Cornbread

Popsicles

Pizza

Toast

Peanut brittle

CRIME AND PUNISHMENT

You did something wrong and you got caught. Your parents believe in discipline. They are going to punish you. It is possible that you can lessen the sentence, if you play your cards right. Try to make provisions for:

Good Behavior:
Criminal lawyers know all about this one. If, in the course of an extended punishment (for instance, being grounded for a month), your behavior is exemplary, the sentence is curtailed.

Hard Labor:
Again, applicable to long-term penalties. You do the dishes every night, and they take a week off your sentence. Of course, they may have decided that your punishment should *be* hard labor ("For that, you are going to clean out the garage!"). In that case, maybe you can negotiate for

Reduced Sentence:
In law courts this is usu-ally granted on the grounds of youth or a first offense. Try to think of a mitigating circumstance in your case (don't bother with "everyone else did it"; parents don't go for that one), like your general good character. "I'll never do it again" is worth attempting; so are tears.

Plea Bargaining:
For use in complicated and serious cases. If your parents are very upset and threaten a terrible punishment, you can try to talk them down by giving them some information they want, like how you sneaked out or where you got the beer.

What to Do with Damaging Information about Your Siblings

1. Blackmail them.

2. Tell.

3. Blackmail them now; tell tomorrow.

I thought it was a *killer bee* and I only wanted to save your *life!*

EXCUSES A PARENT WILL ALWAYS ACCEPT

"I was doing it for school." Parents have an inordinate respect for education. They'll fuss and fume a bit, but then they'll come around.

"I didn't want to worry you." Especially useful when you're very late. "We were kidnapped, but I didn't call home because I didn't want to worry you." This shows a touching concern for your parents' feelings.

"I was looking out for Junior." If you have a young sibling (preferably too young to speak), chasing after him/her is a good excuse for any lapse of attention.

"I just followed the directions. Gee, I'm sorry." For use in domestic mishaps—botched meals, clothes that ran in the laundry.

"I guess I'm not as big/as mature as I thought." This contrite admission will wring their hearts no matter what you've done, and in their haste to bolster your flagging self-esteem, they'll forgive you anything.

THE TELEPHONE

Alexander Graham Bell probably didn't have the faintest notion what he was doing when he invented the telephone. How could he have predicted its enormous significance—not only in terms of worldwide communication, but simply for keeping track of your friends? Imagine—before the telephone, people had to write letters for *everything*.

TYING UP THE LINE

There comes a time in a person's life when it is necessary to talk to their friends daily, at length. Parents do not understand this; you would think the telephone hadn't been invented when they were kids. They tend to get a tad anxious when the line is busy all the time, and when they get anxious they also get mad.

You can always say you were talking about homework, or say that Sally's cat just died and you were trying to make her feel better. They can't object to that.

BREAKING IN ON A CALL

It's easy to break in on a call in your own house—just pick up the extension noisily, and with a stocking held over the receiver (to get that long-distance effect), say in a nasal voice, "This is the operator. Please hang up to receive an emergency call." (Don't do this too often, though, or they'll catch on.)

You can also get your family off the phone by less extreme means. A yell from another part of the house can be very effective; you can pretend to get locked in the bathroom, or that the dog was about to eat the meatloaf. If you get desperate, knock over a chair or drop a plate. Everyone will rush to investigate—and you can sneak off to snag the phone.

STEPS TO ACQUIRING YOUR OWN PHONE

1. Concentrate very hard on tying up the family phone. Let your parents yell at you for at least a week before even bringing up the subject of a phone of your own.

2. Mention that a friend of yours has her own phone.

3. Mention it again.

4. And again.

5. Finally, when your parents yell at you yet *again* about talking in the phone too much, say, "If I had my own phone it wouldn't happen."

6. As a last resort, promise to pay the bills.

DISADVANTAGES ONCE YOU'VE GOT THE PHONE

1. You may have to pay the bills.

2. You will probably have to share it with your siblings.

3. Information may list the phone under "children."

4. Your parents will scream bloody murder if you don't answer it, or if you use the family phone.

SHOPPING WITH MOM

When you reach your teens and sometimes well before then, you'll find that it is no longer enough simply to wear what your mother buys for you. You want a say in choosing what goes on your body. So here you are again, engaged in another battle of the wills. It's going to be especially difficult if you're a small size and can still wear children's clothes, or if you have an older sibling whose hand-me-downs fit you.

The ideal answer, of course, would be to buy your clothes yourself, but it's not always that easy. If you have a job that provides enough money to buy some clothes, great. Then you can simply trot to the store to buy what you need. It's more likely, though, that your mother will look at you at breakfast one morning as you sit there in your favorite old jeans, and then announce, "You need some new clothes." This is the voice of doom—she will not rest until the jeans are not only replaced, but thrown away.

Naturally, your mother will propel you to the stores of her choice, not your own. At *her* store, she will know the salespeople by name and they will discuss you as if you weren't there, so it's important to get her to go where *you* want to. The best way to do this is to claim that it's cheaper.

Things salespeople will make cracks about with your mother:

• your size, whether you're large or small

• your breasts, whether you have them or not

• hair on your chest, whether you have *it* or not

• what you want to buy versus what they think you need

Although most salespeople are eminently untrustworthy, you might be able to find one who's marginally honest. As a test, try on something that's too small or a terrible color for you. The salesperson should agree with you about these points. (His or her clothes are a dead giveaway, too; if he's wearing a mustard-color leisure suit, don't believe a word he says.)

Even if you wind up in your

mother's choice of store and she and the salesperson are choosing the ugliest things for you to try on, the situation's not hopeless. You can be sure that your mother won't buy something that doesn't fit, and you can make sure it won't.

HOW TO FAKE A BAD FIT

Button a shirt crooked

Stand with one shoulder higher so the sleeves look uneven

Twist the legs of pants around so they look lumpy

Stick out your stomach to make a waistband too tight

Your Final Threat

If it looks like you're going to be stuck with something you hate, just say obstinately, "You can buy it, but I won't wear it." Above all things, mothers abhor waste.

Matching Quiz

Match up what Mom is going to say about clothes, with the article of clothing about which she will say it:

"Not until you have something to fill it with."

"But what's wrong with your BVD's?"

"Absolutely not. You'll look like a streetwalker."

"I still think oxfords are much better for your feet."

"That will never keep you warm."

THE FIRST BRA

Even if you don't really need a bra, you should have one so that you have something to stuff. You can't, of course, say this to your mother, so tell her that you want to start wearing a training bra. If she resists, tell her that everyone else in your class wears a bra, and that you're embarrassed to be the only person who doesn't need to. The combination of pride ("my little daughter's becoming a woman") and pity ("I don't want her to feel left out") should propel her straight to the lingerie department of her favorite store, with you in tow.

1. Let your mother do all the talking. That's what she's there for.

2. Agree with everything she or the saleswoman says. This expedition is merely to get over the embarrassment of the first time.

3. Listen carefully to the terms used ("fiber fill, 32AA, seamless cup") so that the next time you can leave Mom at home and simply get what *you* want.

A Note on Stuffing

Cotton is not as lumpy as tissues.

YOURSELF

MANNERS: OR, HOW TO GET WHAT YOU WANT

Sit up straight. Don't talk with your mouth full. Shake hands with Mrs. Marker." If this is the way your mother talks to you, you are probably sick and tired of it. She will tell you that she is trying to teach you good manners, and that manners are important. There is no reason in the world for you to believe her, but in fact she's right. What is important about manners, though, is something your mother may not understand: manners give you power.

Teachers: It may not be fair, but they'll kick up a lot less of a fuss when you're late with your homework; don't go so far as polishing apples, but a friendly glance now and then can take you a long way in their books.

Other Officials: If, by chance, you should ever have an encounter with the law, you will certainly be treated better if you don't give them a lot of lip. It may pain you, but calling a policeman "sir" has been known to have a magical effect.

Relatives: Maybe Aunt Mary *is* crazy. Maybe she *does* have terrible breath. But if you listen to her stories about the Depression, or cut her meat at the table, or play with her yappy dog, she'll notice. It is pitifully easy to become a favorite nephew or grandchild, and the payoff can be considerable.

Parents' Friends: You don't have to hang around and play bridge with them, but it won't hurt to say a polite "hello." Lifelong impressions are formed by such things. Some day you may want this person to give you a job, or to let you marry his daughter. They *never* forget.

Parents of Friends: You should always behave better at someone else's house than you do at home. You should even behave better than your friend does—offer to help with the dishes, laugh at the father's dumb jokes. You will rapidly become a favorite in the house, and they'll always be glad to see you. (This is useful when you want to get out of your own house.) Be careful, though; if Al's parents keep asking why he can't behave more like his nice friend (you), you may not *be* his friend for much longer.

DOS AND DON'TS

1. Do look people in the eye. It makes you seem frank, honest, open, attentive. If you hate eye contact, look at the bridge of their nose. It has the same effect.

2. Call people by their names. You don't have to use the name in every sentence, but use the name at least upon saying "hello." This is incredibly flattering to them.

3. Make sure they know who *you* are. You don't want your brother getting all the credit for your good behavior.

4. Don't worry about dressing the part—the startling contrast between, for instance, a torn T-shirt and a polite greeting can work to your advantage.

5. Do not try any of this on your friends. They will see through you immediately.

HOW TO SAY HELLO

1. How close to stand   2. The handshake grip   3. Smile

73

THE BIKE

The bike is a boon to a teenager; it gives you a measure of independence if you aren't old enough to drive (or if you have trouble getting the car).

Try to choose the right one for you; a bike can say as much about your personality as your clothes do.

To be ridden wearing a baseball cap and jeans—in warm climates, cutoffs and no shirt. This is a boy's bike, or a tomboy's. Important technique: popping wheelies.

Very sensible bike—if you don't care about looking cool. Three speeds, baskets for your books, and the dropped bar means girls can ride it in a skirt. If people tease you, just say, "It's good for commuting." You may look a little like a Girl Scout on it.

Ten speeds, light frame; requires that you use a knapsack and ride bent over. For a dashing unisex image, or for long trips.

No gears, coaster brakes, balloon tires; do not get on this bicycle unless you are desperate. It will do untold damage to your self-esteem.

THE CAR

CALIFORNIA DRIVER'S LICENSE
MUST BE CARRIED WHEN OPERATING A MOTOR VEHICLE AND WHEN APPLYING FOR RENEWAL

EXPIRES ON
BIRTHDAY IN
1990

- NO311465
- FREDRICK PAYNE SQUASH
- 85 BOLINAS ROAD
- FAIRFAX, CA 94930

SEX HAIR EYES HEIGHT WEIGHT   PRE LIC EXP
M   BRN   BRN   5-10   150

DATE OF BIRTH
03-15-70
OTHER
ADDRESS
CLASS 3   3 AXLE HOUSE CAR AND ALL OTHER 2 AXLE VEHS. EXCEPT BUS OR 2
          WHEEL MOTOR CYCLE. MAY TOW VEH. UNDER 6000 LBS. GROSS.

SEE OVER FOR OTHER CONDITIONS.   MUST WEAR
                                 CORRECTIVE LENSES ☐

x Fredrick Payne Squash
3-17-86 CAM M   DO NOT LAMINATE

Having a driver's license is one of the shining goals of adolescence, one of those milestones—like your voice changing or getting your period—that mark the road to adulthood. But unlike many of the ritual milestones, it has a real practical application. A driver's license means nothing less than freedom.

It's just a pity that you have to wait so long to get it, and that you have to go through so much on the way.

Whether you learn to drive at school in a Driver's Ed class, or your parents teach you, it seems certain that the process will be unpleasant. In Driver's Ed they will show you gruesome movies that illustrate what happens when you drive after drinking. They will make you memorize how many yards away from a stop sign it is legal to park, and how long it will take you to brake to a halt when you're driving 60 miles per hour. You do, in fact, need to remember these things just long enough to pass the written part of the driving test, but you know (as the Driver's Ed teachers don't) that you'd remember them much better if you tried to memorize them on the way to taking the test.

If your parents teach you to drive, the process is simplified somewhat; they probably care less about your mastery of the written material than about your mastery of the car. However, since it is their car, teaching you to drive makes them very uneasy. **You must always remember:**

1. Neither one of them wanted to teach you to drive. They probably had a colossal fight about this. The one who lost is the one sitting in the passenger seat.

2. They have forgotten what it was like when they learned to drive.

3. They are *terrified*. They're afraid you're going to kill yourself. They're afraid you're going to kill them! They *know* you're going to wreck the car.

It's no wonder they aren't eager to get into the car with you. Here, as so often, the way around the problem is to act mature and responsible. Don't nag, and don't tease. Don't tell them you should know how to drive in case they drop dead in the car. Don't even think of mentioning that your best friend already knows how to drive. Try the following lines, but at no time should you raise your voice or lose your temper. Remember—you must sound like you're trying to help *them* out.

1. The sooner you can drive, the sooner you can lend a hand with running errands, the carpool, et cetera.

2. It would be a good idea to start learning early so that when you have to drive alone, you're completely comfortable.

❮THE DRIVING LESSON❯

3. (For use only in the North) You should start driving now before it gets snowy—or, you should start driving now while it's snowy, to get used to the bad roads.

When you finally do get your way with a parent, or get into a car with a Driver's Ed teacher, try to be as patient with him as you can. Ignore his right foot pressed firmly to the floor as if he had the brakes on his side. Ignore his hands clutching the dashboard, braced against the collision he is sure is imminent. Don't let him panic you—you are in control. Remember to seem cautious and cool at all times. When you get into the car, buckle your seat belt, adjust the mirrors, pull up the seat. This display of competence will be very reassuring. Always use your turn signals. Come to a full stop at all stop signs. Brake for animals and pedestrians. If you can lull your parent into a sense of security before you get your license, you'll be home free afterward.

While your teacher is in the car with you, never

1. fiddle with the radio. They'd rather you concentrated on the road.

2. drive faster than the speed limit, even if it seems like you're crawling.

3. hang an arm out the window or along the back of the seat. Parents think it takes two hands to turn the steering wheel.

4. do anything stupid like strip the gears or drive with the handbrake on.

5. let on that you enjoy it.

Sorry, Dad, too much accelerator, huh?

Wheeling and Dealing

Learning to drive will not guarantee you instant and complete mobility. Unfortunately, you still have to negotiate for the family car. If you have siblings, this is going to be *especially* difficult, because a sibling is capable of wanting the car *simply* because you do.

1. Weigh your priorities. You would rather use the car for a date on Saturday night than to go to your best friend's house on Saturday morning.

2. Cooperate as much as you can. Do errands for your parents—drive your younger brother to baseball practice or go pick up the cleaning—then take your time coming home. Cruise past your current boyfriend's house, or sneak a cigarette. All the time you'll be getting credit for being helpful.

3. Take it easy. You've certainly heard your parents talking about kids who had accidents the week after they got their licenses. You can be sure those kids weren't allowed to use the family car for *years;* and neither would you be.

MAINTENANCE TECHNIQUES

Or, how to do your share of taking care of the car while making sure everyone knows it.

• Empty the ashtrays one by one, into the kitchen wastebasket, while your mother's cooking dinner. Make four trips from car to wastebasket, and let the door slam each time, to be sure she notices.

• Wash the car early one Saturday morning. Wake your father to find out where the hoses are. Clank buckets, and spray water all over the kitchen windows.

• Before you take the car out ask how much gas there is in it. Make a show of taking out your wallet and counting your money. Hesitate (as if to calculate) and say, "OK, I'll fill it up, then." Put in $3.00 worth.

SLUMBER PARTIES

It's a pity that boys don't have slumber parties—they don't know what they're missing, because a slumber party allows you to combine many of the most enjoyable activities available before you're old enough to drink.

ᕮᕤᖇᕤᖇᕤᖇᕤᖇᕤᖇᕤᖇᕤᖇᕤᖇᕤᖇᕤᖇᕤᖇᕤᖇᕤᖇᕤᖇᕤ

Staying Up All Night

There is a real thrill to being awake at 4 A.M., when nobody else is. The movies on TV are outrageous, and everything seems intensely amusing.

Terrifying Each Other

Everyone's heard the story about the man with the hook on his hand and the couple parked in the woods to neck, but it's still spine-chilling. For best scare value, tell the stories about young girls all alone in big houses on stormy nights.

Gossiping

Gossip is always fun, and the more people contribute to it, the more interesting it will be. (Warning: don't say anything you don't want to have repeated and attributed to you. Slumber parties do *not* usually result in discretion.)

Playing with Makeup

Or hair curlers, or facial masks. Experimenting on other people is much more fun than merely making yourself up. Avoid anything permanent, though, in case you get carried away. It would be mortifying to go to school on Monday if you and all your friends had, for example, the identical hair color.

Discussing Sex

When world leaders do this, they call it an exchange of information—everyone shares their knowledge or talks about their area of expertise, and gradually an accurate picture of the situation emerges. In the case of sex, the picture may not be accurate, but it sure will be interesting.

SNEAKING OUT

This activity is not for the faint-hearted. The whole point of sneaking out is the adventure of *not* being where you're supposed to be; you run the risk of getting caught, and getting sent home, and incurring your parents' wrath. This will be multiplied at a slumber party—the hostess's parents will be embarrassed because they will feel that they are responsible for the kids under their roof. The guests' parents will be embarrassed that their children misbehaved under someone *else's* roof. They will all be doubly furious if you get caught—so don't get caught.

1. Wait until it's really late. If your parents go to bed at ten, they may still be sleeping lightly at eleven. They may even be waiting up to catch you—don't put it past them.

2. Plan your exit route. Avoid the squeaky door, the loose board on the stairs, the window onto the gravel.

3. Make sure you can get back in. It would be really bad if you had to wake your parents up to let you in at 5 A.M.

4. Take the dog with you. He'll provide excellent protection, if you should need it, and the perfect cover—you were just taking him for a walk. And he won't bark the house down when you come home.

5. Watch out for traffic. People who are on the road late at night are likely to be weirdos, drunks, or cops. In which case they might harass you, run you over, or haul you in.

6. No booze. It slows your reactions and makes you careless. The point of sneaking out is getting away with it—liquor lessens your chances.

GROOMING RITUALS

FOR A GIRL

Brushing teeth: twice daily. Three times before dates, followed by Listerine.

Washing: bathing daily. Bath often includes bubble bath or bath oil, and auxiliary activity such as a facial mask. *Duration:* from 20 min. to $1^1/_2$ hours, or until dinnertime.

Facial cleansing: varies according to latest magazine read. Sure to include twice-daily washing, and may encompass such additions as steaming, astringents, creaming, additional washings, scrubs, massages, and, occasionally, prayer.

Hand care: weekly manicures not unusual; nightly application of hand cream, constant inspection of nail polish and evaluation of nail growth likely.

Shaving: see box on shaving legs. Frequent.

FOR A BOY

Ditto.

Washing: shower after sports. Brisk.

Facial cleansing: twice-daily washing with soap and water, followed by anxious examination in mirror for pimples.

What?

Shaving: see box on shaving. Variable from nonexistent to daily; the only constant is the wish that it were necessary to shave more frequently.

SHAVING FOR BOYS

The growth of facial hair is as important as your voice changing, but not—thank God—quite as obvious. Best of all, you can do something about it, like shave. By the time you're thirty you may be tired of shaving every day, but for now the novelty is fresh, and it's tangible proof of adulthood.

DOS

Forget fancy razors. Forget electric, forget triple-track Swedish tempered leather-stropped extra-strong stainless steel blades. Stick to the basics.

Use normal shaving cream. No hot lather, no "fragrance of the sea."

Watch out for pimples.

DON'TS

Use your father's razor, your sister's razor, something old and rusty you found in the medicine cabinet. This is your *face*; mistakes caused by faulty equipment will *show*.

Hurry.

Bother shaving more often than you really need to. If there's no hair there to be shaved off your skin is going to take a beating.

SHAVING FOR GIRLS

Shaving your legs is a complicated process, especially when undertaken for the first time. Like most grooming endeavors, it is best done with a friend for coaching purposes. You will need the following:

1. A bathroom with plenty of room and preferably a door that locks.

2. Shaving cream. Better than soap, which is pedestrian, or hand lotion, which gums up the razor.

3. A reasonably modern razor. Use your father's the first few times so that you can hear him accusing your mother of messing with it.

4. Plenty of toilet paper to stick onto the cuts.

DO NOT PRESS HARD. DO NOT MOP UP THE BLOOD WITH A TOWEL, unless you're prepared to throw the towel away.

83

DIETS

Until you were thirteen or so, you never thought about your weight. You could eat anything with impunity and never get fat. But around seventh grade, several things occur: your body starts to "mature" (as your biology teacher puts it), you have to change for gym, you stop buying children's sizes and start buying clothes in the junior department. And those clothes had better come from the small-size end of the rack. Suddenly the idea hits—maybe you should go on a diet.

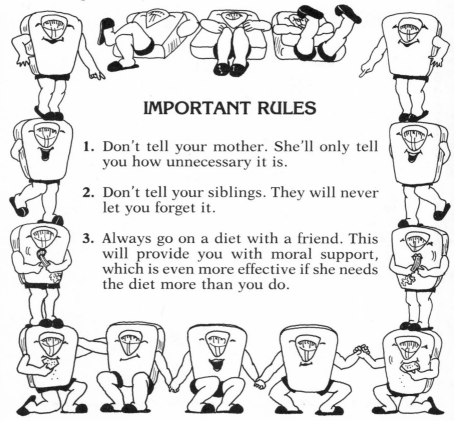

IMPORTANT RULES

1. Don't tell your mother. She'll only tell you how unnecessary it is.

2. Don't tell your siblings. They will never let you forget it.

3. Always go on a diet with a friend. This will provide you with moral support, which is even more effective if she needs the diet more than you do.

How to Choose a Diet

You will probably be on one kind of diet or another for the rest of your natural days, so don't take the choice too seriously. You'll have time to try them all. And they all have advantages.

SOME CHOICES

Counting Calories: gives you a limitless topic of conversation: calorie counts in foods. You can spend hours on the phone with friends discussing how many calories you've eaten that day, and how many you saved by not eating that carrot cake.

Stillman Diet: attracts a lot of attention, especially in the lunchroom. "Is that *all* you're eating?" The amount of water you'll have to drink will make you have to pee all the time—which could be handy for unlimited bathroom passes. Your mother is sure to hate this diet.

Weight Watchers: If you really do need to take it off, this one works, but be prepared for all those meetings (where you will be the youngest and the thinnest person) and the fuss of actually weighing all your food. Good for the scientifically minded.

Low Carbohydrate: If you tire of counting calories (or if you can't add as far as 1,000) switch to grams of carbohydrates. This diet allows foods like peanuts but cuts out potatoes. *Not* good if you already have an acne problem.

Of course, most people don't really lose weight when they diet, and if they do, they gain it back. The real reasons to go on a diet are

1. to demonstrate to your parents that you are too old for them to dictate your eating habits;

2. to do what your friends are doing.

HOW TO TELL
IF YOU'RE OVERWEIGHT

• You hate summer because you have to wear a bathing suit.

• You hate gym because you have to wear a gym suit.

• Salesladies refer to you as "chubby."

• You can't see your feet when you're standing up.

REASONS
NOT TO CARE

1. A hundred years ago beautiful women were much fatter (go to the library to look at pictures of Renoir nudes if you don't believe this).

2. You can eat pretty much what you want; no swearing off chocolate for life.

3. Lots of men admire women with "a little flesh on their bones."

4. Fat is a good insulator against cold. You'd last longer in a blizzard.

HOW TO LOOK TALLER THAN YOU ARE

Everyone knows that girls mature faster than boys. Everyone knows that often girls have reached their full height before boys achieve those last few inches. And of course everyone knows that this can be a real drain on a guy's ego. There are, however, certain steps to take that could help.

• Try a skateboard. It'll add three or four inches.

• Go out for cross-country. If you're running all the time (and you will be), nobody will have time to notice that you're short.

• Cultivate younger women, like eleven-year-olds who haven't started to sprout up yet.

• Dismiss from your mind all thought of elevator shoes. You won't fool anybody. Stick to the sneakers.

• Above all, walk normally. Nothing will give you away faster than a slouch or one of those bouncing walks in which you try to add some height at each step. It's going to look pretty funny when you get to be 6'1".

• Think of Napoleon. Think of Robert Redford. Think of Dudley Moore.

BRACES

When you were little you might have wanted braces so you could be cool. Now that you're older, they don't seem to be all that much fun, but a lot of people have to put up with them.

The Worst Things about Braces

• They hurt. When they stop hurting, they have to be tightened. Then they hurt more.

• You have to spend a lot of time hanging around the orthodontist's office and all there is to read is *Highlights* magazine.

• They're ugly. Don't make the mistake, though, of learning to smile with your mouth closed. You'll be sorry when they're taken off and you want to show off your teeth. If they're *still* ugly, *then* you learn to smile with your mouth closed.

• Things get stuck in them: spinach and corn on the cob especially.

The Tolerable Things about Braces

• You can use them as an excuse not to eat food you don't like.

• Your teeth will be straight so you won't get cavities when things get stuck in funny places.

• You won't have to have them later. They're bad now, imagine how much worse they'd be when you're 25.

• Orthodontist appointments can get you out of school at least once a month.

SOME OF THE COMPONENTS

Night Brace

They might try to get you to wear this to school. Forget it—you know you won't, and so do they. Wear it at home instead, and fiddle with it a lot so your parents feel like they're getting their money's worth.

Retainer

A retainer can create some very interesting effects with water, if you're skillful.(Squirting it, that is.) At the very least you can stick it out on your tongue to disgust your older sister.

Rubber Bands

The perfect missile. If you can't manage to shoot them from your mouth, you can make a teeny sling with them. The target will never know what hit him. Take them out before kissing: in fact, take them out before there's a remote chance of kissing. Only put them back on when you've lost all hope.

MAKEUP

Your parents think you're a child and ought to look like one. You know better—and you want to look as grown up as you can. The fact that there are plenty of 13-year-old fashion models doesn't help your case at all. It is not ridiculous to imagine that, in your parents' eyes, you'll be wearing makeup one minute and the next minute embarked on a career as a child prostitute.

Your principal combatant in this matter is going to be your mother. Your father will simply shrug and say, "You look awfully pretty to me without makeup, honey," and hide behind his newspaper. He would probably not notice if you wore false eyelashes at breakfast. But your mother's eyes are sharp. Of course, she may not object to *any* makeup; it may be that she'll agree to let you wear lipstick when you're fourteen, and blusher to special parties. The point is that she will almost certainly not agree to your wearing as much makeup as you want to wear.

Do not make the following mistakes:

Using Your Mother's Makeup: It's tempting: especially when she's out for the evening and you know she won't be home for hours. But, first of all, it's probably all old-style stuff and will look all wrong and will be hard to get off. Second, you don't want to risk messing it up—breaking a lipstick, scratching a rouge— so that she *suspects* you've been using it.

Using Your Older Sister's Makeup: Older sisters have a seventh sense about these things—she'll know if anything has been touched. She probably isn't above putting hairs on the bathroom shelf (like James Bond) to see if anything has been disturbed.

Doing Anything Drastic: Don't dye anything, or have anything added or subtracted. Plucked eyebrows and tinted eyelashes and permanented hair will not go unnoticed, and even when the storm is past your mother won't trust you.

90

Your goal is to very gradually get your mother used to seeing you with a little bit of makeup on. You don't want a confrontation; you don't want to make an issue out of it. You simply want her to get accustomed to your made-up face, without ever making her consciously aware that your face is—gasp—painted.

1. Buy your own makeup. Keep it somewhere else if she's nosy: in your school locker or at a friend's house. But buy colors that blend in with your skin and things you can use without worrying about getting them off.

2. Do it gradually. Try a little blusher one morning. Your mother will look sharply at you—maybe even ask if you've got anything on. Say you don't, and keep it there. In a week she will have forgotten that's not the natural color of your cheeks, and you can add a little more.

3. Keep it simple. Anything exotic like gold eyeshadow or purple mascara is a dead giveaway. Even your *father* will notice purple mascara

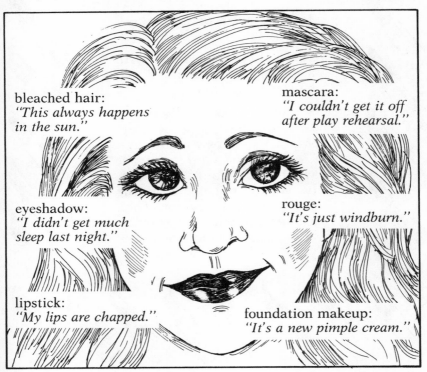

bleached hair:
"This always happens in the sun."

mascara:
"I couldn't get it off after play rehearsal."

eyeshadow:
"I didn't get much sleep last night."

rouge:
"It's just windburn."

lipstick:
"My lips are chapped."

foundation makeup:
"It's a new pimple cream."

Putting On Makeup
in Department Stores

This is a good way to learn what works and what looks awful, how to put on eye pencil and what color blusher you should wear, without raiding your mother's bureau or spending lots of money. However, the salesladies may not look too kindly on your experimentation.

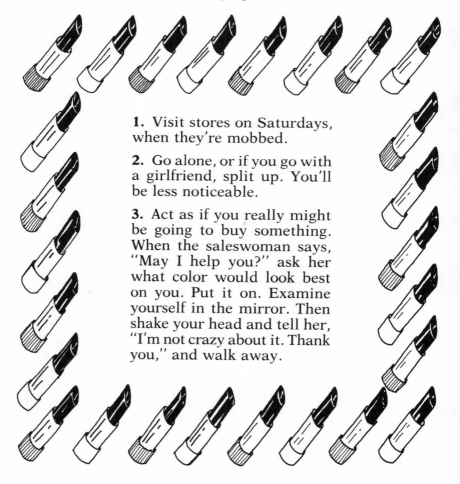

1. Visit stores on Saturdays, when they're mobbed.

2. Go alone, or if you go with a girlfriend, split up. You'll be less noticeable.

3. Act as if you really might be going to buy something. When the saleswoman says, "May I help you?" ask her what color would look best on you. Put it on. Examine yourself in the mirror. Then shake your head and tell her, "I'm not crazy about it. Thank you," and walk away.

CAUTION: HIGH HEELS

A girl's first pair of high heels is a very serious affair. It represents a kind of victory over her parents (who are finally capitulating, since she's been agitating for those shoes for years) and a milestone on the way to being considered an adult. The trouble, however, is this—they can be very hard to walk in. To make it easier:

---

1. Don't go overboard on the first pair; however adult you want to look, spike heels can look ridiculous. They are, moreover, lethal!

2. Scratch the bottoms with a pair of scissors so they grip the ground a *little* bit.

3. Practice before your first public appearance. Walk around the house, and run up and down the stairs until you feel comfortable. Do *not*, of course, let anyone else in the family catch you doing this.

4. Be very careful on stairs, on polished floors, and wearing a long skirt. Keep an eye out for carpets and little steps you might trip on. Any of these could get you, no matter what you have on your feet, but no one will believe it wasn't the shoes.

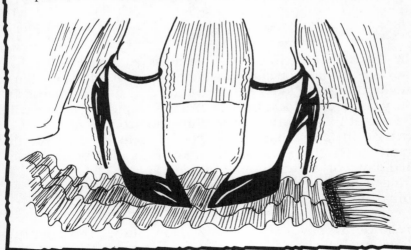

ON KEEPING A DIARY

PRO	CON
You won't ever forget who you were in love with in October of last year.	*Ditto*
It gives you someone to talk to who's even more trust-worthy than your best friend.	*Someone might read it.*
It helps you to remember important events that happen.	*You have to sit down and write about them.*
You can keep track of things and just maybe you won't make the same mistakes twice.	*It is embarrassing to read back and find out what a dummy you were.*

The Actual Book: Since privacy is essential, you can rule out anything that looks like a diary but doesn't lock. Either use one of those leather ones with the little key (hasn't everyone been given one for a birthday?) or write in something deceptive-looking—a spiral-bound notebook, a sketch pad, loose pages stuck in the yellow pages of an old phone book.

Camouflage: It is possible that someone will find your diary anyway, and start to read it. (An unscrupulous sibling will have no trouble getting beyond the lock.) You should make it as difficult as possible.

1. Never, ever, start your entries, "Dear diary."

2. Don't label the opening page, "Anne's Diary, Keep

Out." It will only egg people on.

3. Try writing the first few pages about something else altogether: copy an article about farms out of the *World Book Encyclopedia*. Snoopers will get so bored they'll give up.

4. If you have a turn for this sort of thing, write in code. Then you'll be completely safe and you can leave your diary anywhere. Do make sure you hide the key to the code somewhere, though. You want to be able to read it yourself.

MAKING THE EFFORT

Don't write every day, unless something important happens every day. You'll end up writing down what you had for lunch and what the weather was like, and you'll bore yourself to tears. Some subjects that are usually good copy:

• who you have a crush on, why you like him, whether or not he looked at you today, spoke to you, told your best friend he liked you, kissed you.

• why your siblings drive you crazy.

• how your parents misunderstand you.

• your best friend's crushes and why she is so much luckier in love than you are.

Subjects to avoid, no matter how important they seem or how much you want to write *something*:

• homework.

• the score of the game.

• descriptions of nature, unless they are absolutely essential.

• your pets.

Finally:
If you do keep a diary, do not read back in it. This is especially important for the next few years, when you will be so embarrassed at yourself that you will want to throw the diary away. Once you are 30 (you *will* get to be 30), you would regret this.

HOW TO CRY
WITHOUT BEING
NOTICED

1. Do not cry yourself to sleep. When you wake up, your eyes will be so swollen that you won't be able to see out.

2. Cry in the shower. You can go on for as long as you like and nobody will hear you or notice that your face is wet when you get out.

3. Always wear waterproof mascara. Makeup running down your cheeks is a dead giveaway.

4. Sneeze a few times and pretend your eyes are watering because of allergies.

HOW TO CRY
SO EVERYONE
KNOWS IT

1. Think about something really sad and bite the inside of your lip.

2. Squinch up your eyes to squeeze the tears out.

3. Let each teardrop roll at least partway down your cheek before you catch it.

4. Use a handkerchief, preferably a large one. If you want to make more of an impression, bury your face in it and "sob."

WHY YOUR BROTHER'S FRIENDS DON'T MAKE GOOD BOYFRIEND MATERIAL

Girls who don't have older brothers always envy girls who do, thinking that the older brothers must have friends, and that the friends must always be around the house, and that sooner or later one of them will fall for little sister. This is a fallacy. Just think about the following situations, and how quickly they could hamper romance.

1. It is Saturday morning. Your mother is yelling at you because your hair has clogged the bathroom drain. "You do *not* need to wash your hair every night. And while we're on it, young lady, have you been getting into the peroxide bottle?" You look up to see your brother and your boyfriend standing in the doorway sniggering. You hate them both.

2. You and your girlfriends are talking about how much you hate your brothers and how awful they are. Your friend Susie has just revealed that her brother Ed picks his nose all the time at home. She suddenly remembers that you and Ed are dating, and turns bright red. The conversation ends there.

3. You split your new jeans at a family picnic and you had to go around all day with a sweater tied over your fanny. Your brother can't wait to tell all his friends; there is nothing you can do to stop him.

4. You are dancing with your brother's best friend Joe at a school dance. It is pretty romantic, and you think he might even kiss you. Your brother comes up and says to you in a loud voice, "You better not get too close, Martha; you have bad breath."

Enough said?

BRINGING HIM HOME

Although adolescence is, in general, fraught with potential for embarrassment, one of the most acutely mortifying situations is that of Bringing Home the Sweetheart for Dinner. To mention a few of the obstacles, you'll have to deal with:

Siblings: First, they can tell awful stories about you, how you got carsick last week, how you need to sleep with a nightlight, about the time you cried when you went on the rollercoaster. They can further mortify you merely by being their loathsome selves. It *must* be bad for your image to be related to that funny-looking redhead across the table who keeps talking about his pet lizards.

Parents: They are, potentially, equally dangerous. Why did you never notice the hair growing out of your father's nose? When did your mother pick up that stupid habit of *humming* all the time? Why can't they be like normal parents? (Guess what—they probably are.)

The House: It's an extension of your family, and of yourself. All of a sudden, you think,

"When Peter sees those curtains is he going to think I'm hopeless?" You can probably relax about the curtains, *and* the furniture, *and* your mother's collection of miniature cactus. He won't notice.

As a matter of fact, there's not a lot you can do to prepare for the event. If you have something good to hold over your siblings, blackmail them into silence. (Make sure they *all* agree, though, or one will say something ghastly enough for all of them.) Without appearing to be too anxious you can try to give your mother some advice on what to have for dinner. (You are always safe with chicken.)

It may occur to you that you should try to prepare the guest for this event. Resist the temptation. You don't want to seem too anxious, and coaching your date will give you away. What you *can* do is just say, the day before the dinner, "My family's a little odd." Don't explain, no matter how much your friend presses you to. He or she will imagine all kinds of peculiarities and your family is sure to seem charming in comparison.

KISSING

You are out with a girl you think is pretty attractive. You have been having fun together. You would like to kiss her. Will she slap your face and run away screaming? Burst out laughing? Respond with passion? What do you *do*?

First, calm down. It may reassure you to know that, if you *do* try to kiss her, she won't be surprised. In fact, she has probably been worrying about it ever since you made plans to go out. This actually gives you a huge advantage because if she doesn't want to kiss you, she'll already have thought of ways to let you know it.

1. If you're sitting still, edge over close to her or lean toward her. If she moves away, stop right there. The mobile version of this technique—if, for example, you're out for a walk—is just walking close. (Try not to bump into her.) Bear in mind that, if this is an optional walk and you are not merely going from point A to point B, that's already hefty encouragement. After all, everyone knows what two people do when they're out walking late at night.

2. It's corny, but try the old "one arm along the back of the couch" routine. If she leans back, proceed. If she sits up straight and then gradually relaxes, proceed with caution. If she gets up and sits in another chair, call it a night and go home.

3. Don't bother with holding her hand or any further preliminaries. You both know what's coming, so save the cozy stuff for later. If you're still not sure, just aim for a spot right below her ear and work your way to her mouth from there.

Try to bear the following points in mind:

• Get the first kiss over as quickly as you can without looking like you're tackling her. Neither of you is enjoying the suspense.

• Don't worry if she won't look you in the eye; it doesn't mean that she hates you, just that she's nervous.

• Prepare to forget anything dopey either of you says. You're under a lot of pressure; you can't be expected to be rational.

SHOULD YOU SHUT YOUR EYES?

Yes. Nobody looks good that close.

WHEN SHOULD YOU TAKE OFF YOUR GLASSES?

After the first long kiss, when you've come up for air.

FOR GIRLS: HOW TO DISGUISE BEARD BURN

Don't try to cover it with makeup; use more blusher than usual to get your cheeks and forehead roughly the same color as the rest of your face. Then tell everyone you've been sitting under a sun-lamp.

HOW TO TALK ABOUT SEX

You want, of course, to convey the impression that you not only know all about it but are—well, experienced.

1. Never actually lie. Sooner or later you may be caught in this little deception, and being caught lying is far more humiliating than confessing ignorance.

2. Let other people do most of the talking. Nod knowingly, as if you were comparing your experiences with theirs. Take mental notes.

3. Read a lot. *The Joy of Sex* covers the topic as thoroughly as anyone could want—and it's illustrated, in case your imagination fails you.

4. If you want to ask questions, be careful how you phrase them. Don't say, "What does it feel like?" Say, "Doesn't it feel good?"

5. If someone asks you a question that you don't want to answer, look them straight in the eye and say, "I promised not to tell." They will assume that you promised someone *else* not to tell.

6. Watch your vocabulary—don't use the technical terms you're told in the sex education movies. Current slang is far more expressive.

7. Mention the difficulty of "doing it" in a car with bucket seats.

8. Complain about your back. When someone asks how you hurt it, leer.

9. Discuss your fear that your mother will find your diaphragm, which you hide in your bureau under your sweaters.

10. Worry out loud about the increasing incidence of VD.

11. Always remember that everyone else knows just as little as you do.

SMALL COMFORT

1. If you ask any grownup whether or not he was popular when he was a kid, he'll probably say, "No."

2. Everyone thinks someone (if not 98 percent of the population) is cooler, smarter, more popular than they are.

3. People who reach the peak of their powers at age 14 don't have much to look forward to.

My second-grade picture

Mom. Age 7

1973

1950

Mom at 16 1960

1983

Mom with me on my 17th birthday